MW00477771

WHAT FEELS LIKE LOVE

TOM C. HUNLEY

NEW AND SELECTED POEMS

C&R Press
Conscious & Responsible

Cover art Eugenia Loli
Interior design by Jojo Rita

Copyright ©2021 Tom C. Hunley

ISBN: 978-1-949540-18-5
LCCN: 2020950793

C&R Press
Conscious & Responsible
crpress.org

For special discounted bulk purchases, please contact:
C&R Press sales@crpress.org
Contact info@crpress.org to book events, readings and author signings.

WHAT FEELS LIKE LOVE

TABLE OF CONTENTS

NEW POEMS

(FROM) HERE LIES (STEPHEN FOSTER AUSTIN STATE UNIVERSITY PRESS, 2018)

(FROM) THE STATE THAT SPRINGFIELD IS IN (SPLIT LIP PRESS, 2016)

(FROM) PLUNK (WAYNE STATE COLLEGE PRESS, 2015)

(FROM) OCTOPUS (LOGAN HOUSE PRESS, 2008, WINNER OF THE HOLLAND PRIZE)

(FROM) THE TONGUE (WIND PUBLICATIONS, 2004)

(FROM) STILL, THERE'S A GLIMMER (WORD-TECH EDITIONS, 2004)

New Poems

DEAR GOD, SHOW ME HOW TO WALK IN WONDER

Dear God, when I watched my firstborn
    being born, I thought, at first,
   he looked like a carp, hooked and gasping,
     and I was struck dumb, as silent as You.

My son couldn't speak for years,
    and when the doctor said *Autism*
I couldn't speak, and forgive me,
    I turned my head from him.
I know You'll understand. Forgive me
    for reminding You how You turned Your head
      while Your son hung there.

Sometimes, God, I stumble like a foal,
    a fool, a fawn, a phony. I fail, I fall,
I, who taught, by tall example,
    my children to walk.

Sometimes a wolf steps out of woods
    and I need new words
to ward him off
    because the words I have
      have dried up in my throat.

Dear God, show me how to walk in wonder
    toward You and knock me over
      when I walk away from You
    but let me let my children
     walk away from me.

Just remember the names I gave them:
    She Who Fills My Head And Heart
      With An Unshakeable Ache;
He Who Beats Drums And Beats Me At Ping Pong;
    He Who Slaps The Bass And Cracks The Jokes;

and He Who Ventures Far Into The Cold
To A Place Inside Himself
That No One Else Can Ever Enter.
Not even I can go there,
but I believe You can go there.
Dear God, please go there.

A WORLD INSIDE THIS WORLD

I love watching Bigfoot
in the famous Patterson film,
glance cast over her shoulder
as if at a sudden takeoff of birds,
arms swinging in time to some mysterious
rainforest music, no need to break
stride before returning to her
own thoughts and the ground before her.
So what if all the evidence shows
that she is just a man in a suit?

All the evidence shows that I too
am just a man in a suit,
too hurried to walk like that
or even like the young – unsteady, unsure
where they're going but with years
to get there. My size ten Rockports
already look small next to the size eleven
Converses my fourteen-year-old autistic son
got for Christmas. His enthusiasm for fashion
is legendary, as is his passion for the smallest,
most surprising things. Every day he tells me
how many button-down shirts
he owns (twenty-three at last count).
Every day he says *Guess what,
I've been in high school for 91 days,
92 days, 93 days, 94 days, Wow!*

The heart has many doors, wrote Dickinson
and on the rare occasion when my son lets me in
his room to show me, once again, a Youtube video
of the ten fastest race cars, or to tell me that snakes
move twelve miles per hour, I feel like I've entered
a secret, mythical place, where my son walks tall,
king of everything in shouting distance,

and it's okay to shout in his world,
it's okay to repeat a name a hundred times
because the syllables taste so sweet,
it's okay to bay and rage without pretension
or say just what's on your mind even if it's been there
for months and you've been saying it over and over,
and typical ways of seeing the world
seem like cubic zirconia dreams I've been sold
that keep me from smelling
what Wallace Stevens called the *odor of stars*,
from finding a world inside this world
that is uniquely inhabitable for me.

Then my son says *That's enough*,
that he needs to walk alone, that my
presence threatens to despoil his forest.
I walk out, once again exiled from my own heart,
my GPS signal lost, my contacts gone,
my habitual ways of seeing the world
knocked to the floor like books from a coffee table.
I never would have believed before this
that such a creature could ever exist.

THE LAST TIME I TOOK MY SON TO THE MOVIES

We saw Wonder, the story of a boy
named Auggie with a facial deformity
caused by Treacher Collins Syndrome,
who gets bullied until the other kids
get used to his face and learn to see
past it into his beautiful true self.

My son started talking too loud.
I knew his whole script:
Our car has 162,900 miles on it.
I've saved $304. I'm buying a leaf blower,
some extension cords, some button-down shirts.
They're remodeling my high school
Phase I will begin in 2018.
Phase II will begin in 2020.
They're putting in straight halls
because people get lost in the circular halls.
They should study the interactive map like I do.
How long will this movie take?

The man in front of my son turned and said *Shut up.*
My son's face reddened. He rocked back and forth,
said *You shut up. I'll call the police on you*
as the man tried to lock eyes with him.
I leaned forward and said *Turn around, man.*
The man and I locked eyes with the fiercest looks
we could muster. This lasted forever, a minute, maybe.
We locked eyes for so long that my mind wandered:

>   Will Auggie make friends?
>   What is making that squeaking sound in my Toyota?
>   Should I take it to a mechanic?
>   Who was AC/DC's singer before Bon Scott?

The man pointed at my son and said *One more time*.
I said *Let's go right now*, and he finally turned
back to the screen, where Auggie's dad was telling him
to take off his space helmet and face
the other children staring at his face.

Ten minutes later, my son was still upset,
saying *I'll wreck you* and *You don't do that*.
The man turned again. I leaned forward again,
said *Look, my son has special needs.*
Do you understand that we're watching a movie
about accepting people with special needs?
and my son said *I have autism.*
The man said *Okay. You should have said so before*
and he was right. He and his daughter found other seats.

By the end of the movie, I felt bad
for the man. He didn't know
about my son's inner battles,
and we don't know what he lives with.
Maybe his father had just died,
like Malcolm Young, at age 64,
unable to remember the songs
of his own heart. Maybe he just lost
his job and wondered when he could
afford to take his daughter
to the movies again. I wanted to
take him out for a beer.
I would have listened to him
talk about his father and his daughter.
I would have tried to help him
find a job. But after the movie,
I couldn't find that man among the faces
adjusting to the lights coming on.

WHAT SHE SAID

My son has fallen in love
with *King of the Hill.*
Hank sells propane and
propane accessories, he tells me
for the hundredth time this week.
I laugh like it's the first time, say *Yep,*
tip back an imaginary Alamo beer.

You sell poetry and poetry accessories
he says, and I laugh for real.
And people with no sense say people
on the spectrum have no sense of humor.

He's having more trouble with
"That's What She Said."
How was school today?
    That's what she said.
Have you fed the dog?
    That's what she said.
For some reason this upsets me.
I tell him it's only funny in context.

I show him the episode where Ben Stiller
guest stars as the voice of Rich,
a new Strickland Propane employee
with a potty mouth: *I need an 8-inch L-pipe.*
    That's what she said.
I hope this drill has enough juice for the job.
    That's what she said.

My son gives me the same lost look
my college freshmen get when we come to lines
like "making the beast with two backs."

I collect myself.

Son, I say. *I don't care if you never understand bawdy humor.*
Or why I like metaphors so much.
You are the one program I could watch all day
without changing the channel.
I just want you to be happy in this life.
  That's what she said, he says,
tilting his head in his mother's direction.

REMEMBER THOSE GIRLS, LORD

Remember all those profiles of teen girls
in foster care, how we grieved
that we could only bring one home?
Remember those girls, Lord,
how the social workers advised:
this one bit her foster siblings
and is on lockdown; this one lit
a firecracker under a sleeping cat
and will soon age out of the system;
this one has falsely accused men and boys
in three foster homes and will ruin
your reputation; and this one (the one who
joined our family, thank you Lord)
ate shoplifted groceries with her
siblings as their birth mother
nodded off under the spell of heroin
and both men in her home
were unregistered sex offenders.

When she confessed to sneaking
onto our computer at night, encouraging
some boy to send dick picks
to her secret social media page,
how I raged, angry at him, afraid
for her. Lord, only You know
how many men and boys have shown her
their ugly sides. Composing myself,
I told her never to send pictures of her
body, but if she did, never to include her
face, because porn is a thing
and revenge porn is also a thing.
Thank You for keeping her off drugs –
but help me to see her
as myself at her age,
trembling in the county detox ward,

waiting for a room to open up
in a rehab center, and help me
be like the junkie I met there,
who said *Hey, I only have one cigarette,*
it's really all I have, but why don't you take it?

WHAT FEELS LIKE LOVE

What if I could bottle my daughter's joy
at the Bruno Mars concert   as she gleamed
I love this song as he sang   *although it hurts*
I'll be the first   *to say I was wrong*
from her favorite song   except for "The Girl is Mine"
Michael Jackson/Paul McCartney in pop tug-o-war

Adoption means the girl is mine   so when a dirtboy
asks her to penetrate herself with a pencil
while he watches on Skype   I hiss at him
like a rabid raccoon and his family moves out of town

When another dirtboy talks her into photographing herself
topless   before a mirror   and putting it on Snapchat
I say *You don't have to be nice to people who aren't nice to you*
and she says *Dad, he said 'please'*   *that's being nice, isn't it*
and I can't even   sleep without pills for a year

What feels like love is often   a lie a boy tells
          a lie you need to learn to smell   *Be mine* I say
A father is a magic mirror   that shows you
your beautiful true self   I've never had a daughter before
but I've had sons   changed diapers coached
          t-ballsoccerbasketballfootballtennis

Her mom and I wanted her
          the way sunlight and water want grass
When she says she can't won't live   without some dirtboy
I feel like a gimpy superhero   flying but not fast enough
to protect her from her own confused heart

A father is a tree that hangs onto its leaves
as long as possible   holds them high as they turn beautiful colors
Dad   *a new boy has a crush on me*   she gushed
and I had to ask   *does he have a crush*   *Sweetie*
          or did he hear you'll have sex
without even a movie date first   The girl is mine mine mine

19

Zero degrees outside icy 5:30am   I see a boy bicycling
        out of our driveway   He lives across town
I knew he would do that for me she says   What feels like love
is abuse   when a boy talks her into
giving him all her passwords to prove she's not cheating

A father is a parachute   that lands you safe as raindrops on a lake
Adoption means the girl is mine   Be mine
a gold mine a treasure   Be mine because I cry when you cry
Be mine because I fear for you   when you don't
        have the sense to fear for yourself
What feels like a punch in the nuts   is really love
when you love a girl   who doesn't know
yet   how to love herself

POUNDS

Our eighteen-year-old daughter cringes,
scowls at the scale. *Mom, I weigh 1290,*
she shouts, her voice pained by a world
that's had its foot on the scale ever since
she was born, freighted with the weight
of her birth mother's drug addiction.

It's a digital scale, Sweetie,
says my wife. *You weigh 129.0.*

Our daughter bounds down the stairs
to where her brothers and I
are spilling soda and chips
as the Seahawks fly past the Eagles.

Dad, I lost pounds, she says.
We clap and cheer. *How many pounds
did you lose, Sweetie?* I ask.
I don't know. I weighed 133.
Now I weigh 129, she says.
So what's 133 minus 129? I ask.
I don't know, she says,

and I don't know what the adoption blues are
except twelve bars that I fear I'll keep
repeating longer than I can keep counting,
and I don't know if she'll ever leave home,
and I hope I can be someone she can count on,
that I can carry this weight which feels
ten times heavier than my own body.

WILL BE DONE
(for Will Brown)

You were my student and I failed you.
And I've failed others.
After I heard of your death, I failed a freshman

for coming to class late blasting Kendrick Lamar
through cheap headphones during a reading
of "Do Not Go Gentle Into That Good Night."

Did you rage as day broke with its peach light, Will?
Sometimes, to write a poem, you had to go places
so dark and so silent you fell and kept falling.

On your way back to yourself,
you got lost and we lost you.
We missed you during the final, Will.

Nothing's more final than this death.
Will, this poem isn't really for you.
It's for everyone left.

I'm using a device called *apostrophe*.
As if you're the urn, not the ashes.
As if you're Autumn, not the fallen.

But you knew that already.
We covered it in class.
While you were still with us.

Before I smelled booze on your breath.
At two pm. Outside my office.
Before the incompletes.

Before your freshmen complained that you kept missing class.
That they missed you. I miss you.
Your life was incomplete, Will. You didn't fail.

Will you wake in a sky full of stars?
Will it feel strange not having the darkness you're used to?
The darkness you used to carry everywhere?

There's light in this puddle and my face in this puddle
and when I step, there's a splash and the light goes away
and my face goes away but both return.

The light will never return to your face.
Your face will never return
to any puddle or mirror or classroom.

Everybody left came back.
You left and will not come back.
The bullet left the gun like curses from a mouth

that would eat them whole to take them back, but can't.
I'm fighting my demons, you wrote to me.
You lost your way and your battle and you broke

like one of your bottles, spirits spilling
out of every shattered, unswept piece of you.
I lost Nashville and Tennessee in my rear view mirror

and stanzas I wrote in my head but not on paper
and you, lost like Atlantis, like an old man's memories,
like a wallet, snatched away on the first night in a city far from home.

I never bought that PRS Starla we checked out together
at Royal Music, and now I never will.
You said *It's expensive.* I said *It's overpriced.*

You said *I could never afford it.* I said *My wife would never allow it.*
But we both loved the bird inlays on the fretboard.
Now when I visit the music store, the birds

shriek as if impaled, kabobbed.
If I touch the guitar it will scream
every caged sound you never let out.

Every day now I listen to David Bowie sing
"Rock And Roll Suicide." *You're not alone*, he sings.
I wish I'd said that. *I've had my share,* Will.

There's a D9 chord in that song, Will.
I wish you were here to show me how to finger it.
You and your girlfriend never did come over for dinner.

Now you never will. My wife makes this teriyaki steak.
It tastes amazing. It tastes like love feels.
It tastes like the most beautiful song you ever heard.

I just re-viewed *Pump Up The Volume*.
Christian Slater's underground DJ character talks on air
with a suicidal teen. The next night

he lights candles, plays "If It Be Your Will"
by Leonard Cohen, and weeps: *I never said "Don't do it."*
I never said that. I never said *You're not alone.*

I'm not really talking to you, Will.
I'd just as well talk to the West Wind or an artichoke.
Everyone left, I'm talking to you. Don't leave.

You're not alone. You're not alone. You're not alone.

(from) Here Lies (Stephen Foster Austin State University Press, 2018)

HERE LIES TOM C. HUNLEY, ON HIS HAMMOCK

swinging between two oaks
between the danger of a stinger
and shocks of silence
between his shadow sprawled out
on his long-neglected lawn
and the twilit sky bruised
like the eye of a boxer knocked down
and fighting his way back up
who, upon rising, sees his body
still sprawled on the canvas
looking so serene he forgives himself
finally for not being a champion
for letting his father flatten his mother
over and over until he found the combination
that unlocked his fury and cold-cocked his father
and who, gazing somehow into his own
dazed eyes, sees that there's more
to a person than he could ever fit
in his fists, more than he could hold
clenched in his muscled oiled arms
more beauty than you can bottle
in something as soft and lightweight
as a body

HERE LIES TOM C. HUNLEY, WHO, ACCORDING TO THE CORONER,

held traces, in his blood,
of somethingwrongwithhimhardtosaywhat,
and if you had asked him,
he would have said he had a chronic case
of feeling like a guitar string that busted
and came to think of itself
as a strand of white hair that floated away

He knew love felt like a color with no name
that only one other person could see

He knew loneliness, too; it wore a mask
that made it look like love

Do you think the bluebird over your shoulder is singing

It's telling you to watch where you're going,
and where you're going is telling you
not to go there in such a hurry

HERE LIES TOM C. HUNLEY, KILLED IN A CAR WRECK

by a cop chasing a 2am drunk driver

The cop's face kept turning blue
then disappearing as his light flashed
and the screams of his siren
swirled above this scene
that no amount of yellow tape
could un-Humpty Dumpty

Dying, Tom C. Hunley saw moonlight
as soft and pale as a breast,
muttered *moonlight as soft*
and pale as a breast
felt the mouthful of syllables
and suckled

HERE LIES TOM C. HUNLEY, WHO DIED IN THE SHOWER,

just dissolved, dripped down the drain

Once he ate candy so sweet
he had to change his name

Once he stepped into a silence
so thick it made his legs wobble

Once a song lodged itself inside him
made him so new that when
he called out to his old self
his old self didn't recognize him
and ran off afraid

Death is a pirate that opens your chest
steals everything shiny

As a child, Tom feared the dark
not knowing what it held

As a man he plunged into it
still not knowing

TOM IGNORED THE WARNING LABELS

Warning, said the ground,
subject to periodic earthquakes

Warning, said a leaf,
turning brown and browner
teabag dipped in boiling water

Warning, said the fence between love
and loss, *we will both fall*

Warning, said a crushed aluminum can,
I was full and bubbly an hour ago

Warning, said a bouquet of helium balloons
that he bought for his date at the fair,
we'll fly away from her

Too busy or lazy to heed these signs
Tom ignored his skin
discoloring like a spoiled pear,
the years gone like pages
wadded up and backspinned
into a wastebasket

Even if he'd read the warning labels
the years would have rocked him;
he'd still feel them like you feel
an amusement park ride after stepping off

WATCH TOM FREEZE TO DEATH

Tom C. Hunley leapt off the bridge
between a bridge and the word *bridge*—
sturdy enough to give the word meaning
and the structure a name, not unlike
the name Tom C. Hunley, itself
a bridge between an aggregate of letters
and a man of letters whose hair turned
white and blew off—picture seed fuzz
floating away from a weed—no, picture
snow, now picture Tom C. Hunley
leaping off an actual bridge
only to land on snow and then
the desire to die thaws as life begins
to almost make sense again as he imagines
almost connecting with other people
the way some words almost rhyme—
forever and *moreover* for example
so he decides he wants to live forever
and moreover it seems possible
but then he sees blood on snow
feels his knees going on strike
screams *I can't get up*
as the sky darkens and the ground
hardens and his words echo
off the ice, coins tossed
to the ground from a bridge

TOM'S DEATH WITH A DAVID BOWIE SOUNDTRACK

Somewhere out there, like the truth
floats Major Tom C. Hunley
helmet on, engines on
thrilled to star in a David Bowie song
but why couldn't it be Ziggy Stardust
or China Girl or even Let's Dance

He could have been clubbed
by a wannabe hero or he could have
been hunky dory instead of sitting
in this tin can,

Each of his molecules misses his wife

They miss soil and wish
for a proper burial

They miss stones that sit still
as if posing for photos
unlike these asteroids
that knock on his space craft
and then ricochet away
like disappointed trick-or-treaters

Major Tom C. Hunley rose and vanished
like vapor on a lake
or like birdsong
in a sky so dark
even Death says a little prayer
and a curse word or two
while fumbling for a light switch
that isn't there

SURROUNDED BY ALIENS

Who isn't a baby in a blanket
thrown out the window of a burning house

Who isn't a bamboo kite about to be torn to pieces by a flesh-and-
blood kite

Who isn't a windstorm embarrassed to ask for directions
but also afraid to subside

Tom C. Hunley lies
in a hospital bed surrounded by aliens—
his family and friends but from a different world
from the one where he lies
snapped like branches and then burned
like branches and then overwhelmed
like a small flame by the soothing music of rain

He's not gone or quite still here but in between
like all of us always in between

Who isn't a house with many rooms
all of them hallways

Who isn't surrounded by aliens
wondering why war looks like love
why love looks like war

Hello hello says the nurse like a question spat into a telephone
while she touches him and he hears but can't tell her
her touch makes him feel too much
like food that cries each time it's bitten
in a voice like a dog whistle and so ouch
so much ouch but the nurse's beauty
stings, a sunset seen from a prison cell

(from) The State That Springfield Is In (Split Lip Press, 2016)

EDNA KRABAPPEL

Am I the worst teacher ever?
I will not waste chalk.

If I have the guts to leave the teaching profession and open that muffin store,
I will finish what I sta

What if the substitute is smarter and prettier than I am?
I will not yell "She's Dead" during roll call.

If only my husband had been a better husband or our marriage counselor had been
a better marriage counselor or the two of them weren't so cute together.
Cursive writing does not mean what I think it does.

What if I wrote letters to their doctors asking to excuse them from checkups?
I will not prescribe medication.

If I wear a short skirt to work, will Seymour want to see more?
I will not conduct my own fire drills.

If Bryn Mawr College mostly just taught me to fake it in bed and in the classroom,
I will not belch the National Anthem.

Can't they get their sex education at home?
I will not do that thing with my tongue.

What can I do for the child with bruises on his psyche but none on his arms?
I was not touched "there" by an angel.

If I smell chalk everywhere I go,
I am not Charlie Brown on acid.

If the students grow up to cheat on their taxes and their spouses the way they do
on their tests,
I will only provide a urine sample when asked.

Will they realize how under fire I feel, how one against thirty?
Over forty and single is not funny.

If I secretly root for the boy with ADD and against the twin girls with all the answers,
"March Madness" is not an excuse for missing school.

Do my students know how little I make?
I will not charge admission to the bathroom.

Can we get rid of all the ribbons and teach self-confidence instead of self-esteem?
They are laughing at me, not with me.

OFFICER DOWN
(Police Chief Clancy Wiggum)

This dream keeps screaming
at me. I'm cleaning up the sweet
illegal fireworks that I confiscated
and blew up. I can tell
that one of them remembers me
leaving it sputtering on the ground.
It says *Why'd you light me*
if you couldn't ignite me?
and it has Ralphie's face.

He's always delighted
in long things:
hoses, extension cords,
suspenders. *Dad, let's walk the dog.*
I'll hold the leash and we'll look at the power lines.
Sure, son.

I made him goalie of The Mighty Pigs,
but he brawled all by himself and
skated figure 9s and figure 7s,
laughing at his own visible breath,
saying *I'm a freezer.*

He rode every roller coaster at Praiseland,
then spent a hundred hours watching
Youtube videos of those coasters
and hundreds more drawing
detailed pictures of them. Me,
I won't even go on the Ferris wheel,
and boy does that boy make me dizzy.

What did you do in school today?
Square danced.
Oh, in gym class.
No, in the cafeteria. Some kids cheered. Some threw food. I had fun.

39

I hear the other kids laugh at him
when I swing by after school in my cruiser
and I wish I could cuff 'em and book 'em.

Ralphie spins, says *I'm the world,*
and he is, he's my world that feels
alien sometimes, spinning far away from me.

TROY MCCLURE

Hi, I'm Troy McClure. You may remember me
from such films as *Suddenly Last Supper*
and from such do-it-yourself videos
as *Dig Your Own Grave and Save.*
And I need prescription glasses – bet
you didn't see that coming. Neither did I.
You may even remember me from long before
my starring roles in such self-help videos
as *Smoke Yourself Thin* and such medical films
as *Mommy, What's Wrong with that Man's Face?*
Do you remember? I measured your boyfriend's
inseam and rented him a fitted tux before you lost
your virginity on prom night. We went to
twelve years of school together. Do you remember?
You said my cologne smelled like jasmine
and sandalwood mixed with gym locker.
Now I've got my own scent, *Smellin' of Troy.*
You may remember me. Part of my job
at Burger King was refilling toilet paper rolls
in the restrooms – sorry I didn't knock.
You may remember me. I drove a float
in the Springfield Parade. You wore your crown,
your sash, and your gown as you waved
and blew kisses at everyone but me.
Remember? I hauled the Marshalls
and tested the microphone for the band
that played your wedding reception.
You may remember me. I wore a tiny
red, white, and blue thong to the beach,
hoping to lure me some fish.

MOE SZYSLAK

Hello, Listen Lady? Uh yeah, this is
Moe, of Moe's Tavern. See, I tell you
my name up front, cuz I don't want you
to confuse me with one of them
prank callers. We got one of those
at the bar, a scum-sucking pus-ball
who makes me say stuff like
"Is there a Drew P. Weiner in the house?"
I get so mad, I want to take
a bottle opener to his veins
and then dunk him in the shark tank
at the Springfield Aquarium. Listen, lady,
I want you to teach me to give advice
like a bartender ought to be doing.
Sure, I can offer a trusty Duff,
a Flaming Moe, or the best watered-down
scotch around, but if the chaser is me
mocking the poor barhound's necktie,
I'm not doing my job. I'm always fightin'
with myself, that's my problem. I'm part Dutch,
part Italian, part Arab, part Polish, and
it feels like all these parts are at war
inside my bloodstream. Somehow you just gotta
surrender to your own complexities, like that poet
who said "I am large, I contain multitudes."
I wish I'd thought to say that to this egghead from
Springfield Heights Institute of Technology who
comes in one night, back when Moe's was a
Pomo joint called M. He tells me he's teaching
classes in women's literature where he and his
charges spit out the word *patriarchy* as if
dislodging a chicken bone, and he's careful
not to point out that he's the family breadwinner,
he does most of the driving, and he
spanks the kids if he gets a call

from their principal. So he's a feminist professor
and he's a patriarch. He can't get along
with himself, so he drinks. Why do people turn
to barkeeps for advice, anyhow? Is this
the mug of a guy who knows what's what?
I mean, I moved to this here burg cuz
the zip code spells "boobs" if you type it
on a calculator. My bar's such a girl repellent
that I never even needed to put in a Ladies' Room.
Still, they tell me their girl troubles.
Me, my last girlfriend left me, and she
was a blowup doll. Stupid helium. I don't want
you to think I'm a bad guy or nothing, though.
Sure, I stalk my friends' wives, and I guess
running that whale smuggling ring wasn't
my finest hour, but I love my cat, Snookums.
That's got to count for something, right?
Once I saved music store owner King Toot
from a burning Chevy, and on my nights off I've been
reading *Little Women* to them sweet little hospital urchins.
I've got a soft spot for kids when they ain't crank yankin',
asking if there's a Hugh Jass on any of my barstools.
Do you ever fight with yourself, Listen Lady?
I mean maybe you're a snake handler,
like me, but some days you just don't
believe in nothin'. Take it from me, an ex-boxer,
when you fight with yourself,
you're gonna lose, bet on it.

PROFESSOR JOHN FRINK

I'm Professor Frink. I'll make
you laugh. I'll make you
think. I'll make a thing
that will make you love me.

Oh holiest of Gods, I prayed one day,
with the wrath and the locusts and the
fish swallowing your servant whole
but also with the starry promise
to Abraham and the sealing
of the lions' mouths in the den,
make me a maker, like you.

As a sign the Lord gave me a rose
with the sad red beauty and the
fragrance and the thorns that prick you
when you pluck it – an offering
to a pretty girl – with the sweaty palms
and the shaking fingers and the voice
cracking like a vase.

As another sign the Lord sent a southbound
flock with the feathers falling like rain
and the perfect choreographed vee pattern,
and lo, a great wind blew through the grass
and rocked the street lights and I heard
the voice of the Lord sing the song
of the world and reveal the key
to the mysteries, which I received
like a stick of gum with the sweetness
and the chewiness and the bubble
popping and sticking to your face.

Experiment after experiment
blows up in my face,
science turning on me the way
the robot body guards I made
turned on Mr. Burns.
I blew up Moe's while trying
to knock a comet from the sky,
but in time I will find the formula
that translates the holy word of God,
which lives on the tip of my tongue
and which I hold the way, I am told,
a beautiful woman holds smoke
in her mouth, savoring it in
the exalted moment after making
love in tall grass under a well-made sky.

OTTO MANN, INTREPID BUS DRIVER

One time, when I was blotto, my Converses
started talking to me. If I could explain
what they said, if I could find words

to match the road's wordless language,
you would learn more than your teachers
could put on a year's worth of chalkboards.

I'll get you to Springfield Elementary, but
we're taking the scenic route, scenesters.
Look to your left at the forest fire.

The whole world's burning, that's your first lesson.
You can get a tattoo in this town
on your fourteenth birthday,

and you should. That's lesson number two.
Get out your air guitars to see how
many kinds of silence you can pluck

out of the air. Somebody give us a beat —
you, Dolph, make a scratching sound
like a broom sweeping a house,

and you, Kearney, try to sound like
a wind blowing in a place
where there are no houses around,

while Jimbo makes a scraping sound,
like someone raking leaves.
I'm going to teach you all

a new word: *intersubjectivity.*
I learned that at Brown University, where
I almost made tenure. It means

the silence of those trees connects
to the silence of your air guitars.
It means my thoughts and yours

can meet mid-air, without us having to speak,
if we let it happen. I remember school,
recess spent alone looking at the parking lot,

wet and shining, the yellow sounds
of the buses calling me, telling me
the clouds overhead were a blueprint

for a heaven still under construction.
I wanted to translate those sounds.
Sometimes I think this bus will lift off

and take us to that half-finished heaven.
I feel myself drift away from this world.
I fall into a sleep as deep as the sleep

of the dormant notes inside my Les Paul,
and I wake just before the bus goes off a cliff,
seeing dawn's reddening light and the tall grass

gone greener than any green light, and I realize
that each of us is just a little breath,
that this yellow school bus is a canary

sent deep into the mines, that you
are the precious shiny metal in those mines,
that you are the sunlight sparkling

on the Springfield river as the road bends
and the bus hugs the road and the world awaits
the honking of our horn, the screeching of our brakes.

GOODNIGHT MILHOUSE

(Luanne Van Houten, née Mussolini)

Once there was a special little guy who put on his big boy pajamas and promised not to wet the bed. Mommy called him Sweet Little Treasure but he said *I want to live with Weekend Dad* so he was sent to bed without eating any non-dairy, peanut-free snacks.

The boy started to cry but he was allergic to his own tears and pretty much everything else. *If you leave to live with that rotten, change purse-carrying loser, said Mommy, I will have Pyro punch your dad and bring you back, for you are my Sweet Little Treasure.*

I will become a boat and sail to my father, said the boy.

If you become a boat, I will send my ex-boyfriend, The Sea Captain, to bring you back to me, for you are my Sweet Little Treasure, said Mommy.

Weekend Dad and I will leave Springfield in the middle of the night, said the boy.

If you and your weakened dad steal away from Springfield, I will have him charged with kidnapping, and Chief Wiggum will have Lou book him, said his Mommy, *for you are my Sweet Little Treasure. Besides, what would you eat? Your father can't even keep a job as a bean crop scarecrow or as an assistant to the guy who puts fliers under windshield wipers.*

That very dark night the boy fell asleep while listening to Jimi Hendrix sing "Wild Thing" and in his dream, he sailed to a forest full of everything groovy. School bullies lived in the forest, and when the boy saw them, his heart sang the saddest song of all. The bullies swore their terrible swears, gnashed their cavity-filled teeth, and showed the dirt beneath their fingernails. *We'll beat you up,* said Nelson. Then the wild rumpus started, and the bullies gave the boy wedgie after wedgie until he went back to Mommy's loving arms. She kissed him and hugged him and said *I'll never let you go; I'll never let you grow.*

HERMAN HERMANN,
OWNER OF HERMAN'S MILITARY ANTIQUES

They can take our guns, but we'll still have
water ballons. They can fake a lunar landing,
but I'll still be standing on the dark side.
They can take our cigarettes, but I'll keep
sucking air. Want a fez hat worn by Napoleon?
An authentic pair of Nazi underwear? I lost
my arm in the ball return at Springfield Lanes.
Check out my self-published *Dictionary Code*.
Webster's included all the words, all the meanings.
I tell you how to arrange them so that you'll know
what I know, which will blow your head
clean off your head, the way dynamite blew
my arm off. Here's the hat McKinley had on
when they offed him. I'm not blinking.
That's how you know I'm not lying.
I never blink, not since I stuck my arm out
a bus window and an animal control truck
tore it off like a leaf from a tree. Care for
a shoebox containing the heart of John Keats,
signed and certified? I sleep with both eyes open,
a phantom finger on the trigger. You think
I'm crazy? That's what they want you to think.
Here's an A-bomb built for Ike
to drop on a beatnik coffeehouse.
They put a chip in my brain so they could see
my dreams, but they can't take my dreams.
You're not buying this? Listen to you.
Your voice sounds like a lamb's bleat
just before a lion eats it. Beat it.

"JIHADIST HOMER,"
AN EPISODE FOX WAS TOO CHICKEN TO AIR

(Lisa Simpson)

As the opening credits roll, Osama Bin Laden hides
behind our couch, his big eyeballs zig-zagging
like flies wary of the swatter. Then I'm the fly
and Ralph Wiggum and Milhouse are the swatters.
It's Valentine's Day at Springfield Elementary,
and first Ralph stacks the Hallmarks on my desk,
I choo-choo-choose you superimposed on a train, for one.
Then the bell rings, and I run from Ralph right into Milhouse,
his lips cherry-chapsticked and puckered into a heart shape.

I run right past the school bus and Otto Mann's *Catcha later
little chica* and duck into the new Springfield Islamic Center.
The women and men in there sit on opposite sides of the room
just like the kids on the school bus, but these men
aren't making obnoxious offers of chocolate and roses.
I buy a hijab and a Koran, thinking modesty will turn off
those pesky boys. *I'll be in my room*, I tell the family,
and when Dad comes up to summon me to dinner,

the holy book falls open to Surah 8, Verse 60
as reading glasses appear suddenly on his face:
*Prepare for them whatever force and cavalry you are capable of gathering
to strike terror*
to strike terror into the hearts of the enemies of Allah and your enemies.
I tell him that *Islam* means *Peace* and most American Muslims are good,
moderate, taxpaying citizens, but Dad says *Woo hoo* and something
about getting a Ramadan holiday from his job at the nuclear power plant
and he runs out to join a radical-bearded sect. *Hmmm*, says Mom

when Dad's new friends refuse the BLTs she offers
and put Dad up to giving her a chador as a Valentine's Day present.

After dinner, Nelson taps on my bedroom window, and I let him in
because he reminds me of James Dean and because he's carrying
a three-foot-tall stuffed Cupid. He strips off my hijab, says *haw haw*,
and tickles me on my bed. After one of Dad's new friends happens by,
looking for The Men's Room, they decide to stone me!
Eat my shorts, says Bart, and pulls down his pants,
revealing a Danish Mohammed cartoon stenciled on his boxers.

Dad strikes a deal: we get spared and he agrees to suicide-bomb
Mayor Quimby's office. In the closing scene, Dad's in the afterlife
with his seventy-two virgins, and he sees why they're still virgins.
It's Crazy Cat Lady, our chain-smoking Aunt Selma, Lunchlady Doris,
Comic Book Guy's twin sister, Ms. Albright the frigid Sunday School teacher,
and a bunch of others you don't even want to know about. Dad's annoyed grunt
reverberates all over heaven and earth and the closing credits.

(from) Plunk (Wayne State College Press, 2015)

UM

Often I'm awakened by awful noises:
jackhammers, dynamite, walls crumbling
and bigger ones climbing the sky
in their places. My future arrives and I
have to settle for it. I don't understand how
I got here any more than a lobster understands
how it ended up in a tank next to a *Please Wait*
to be Seated sign, but both of us can read
the faces of the cruelly beautiful women
who point at us. I always feel eyes on me,
so I apologize to insects after I kill them
and to the salmon on my plate, caught
being nostalgic for home. Everything looks clear
if you squint just right, and at least once a day
I realize that whatever I've been saying
isn't the point at all. I spend most days listening
to other people almost making sense, and I don't
ask them what the hell they're talking about
because they're on television or the radio or
because I'm eavesdropping from the next table.
When I'm not talking or listening, I'm in a
boil, my shell softening. I'm getting a good look
at a wrecking ball. I'm crumbling.
I volunteered for all this, accidentally,
by raising my hand, intending to ask
a question I couldn't put into words.

WHAT CAN BE SAID ABOUT THE
BEAUTIFUL-FROM-A-DISTANCE ELEGANT ETCETERA
IN THE BROKEN SYLLABLES OF OUR IMPERFECT
TONGUES?

In our lust for lists and our need
to name, what sense there is
to be made gets made and unmade
like a bed, and we are both
the despairing maid and the young boy,
ecstatic to have tousled it
into a senseless mess like strewn wildflowers
he would bouquet for her if he
were older. Umbrella eaves and
the darkening of sky, we contain both
of these, the little black-keyed symphony
that begins with a note of despair
and ends with heartcries of flesh
and longing and morning after sighs
and the great convulsive sadness of knowing
that we never could love as we should love.
I have been spared the unspeakable sufferings
that the newspapers shout out daily,
so I can't truly know the greatest joys
and gratitudes, and I'm grateful not to know.
I'll buy you flowers before you're buried
in posthumous praise. Casting its light
in this beautiful park, the sun rests on
our skin. Nothing more remarkable has ever happened.
Home is where the heart attack is.
I'll buy you a drink before one of us,
in our clumsy fumbling, breaks.
The heart attack wants what the heart attack wants.
I have been singing happy songs
into your mouth for the mere pleasure
of listening when you lift them
back to my ears, those ditches

where so many silly voices have dumped
so many silly words. The maid, tired
from scouring other people's houses, spanked
the spoiled rich boy silly and his parents fired her,
their blue blood boiling. A hinge that opened the door
to a better life, it turned out, for it forced her
to go to college, get an MBA, become a CEO.
If you're wondering whether their paths
crossed again, that's good, wonder being
central to poetry. Anyone who has ever
felt nervous or awkward in a crowd but comforted
to learn it's only part of some larger nervousness
spreading in the crowd like The Wave, or any scarred body
that has ever felt marred beyond hope of beauty, lodged
in a bottle, lost in an antidepressant fog yet still praising
naked infinite possibility knows what I'm talking about.
The swervings of the heart. The remarkable change
of the sky from hour to hour. That sort of thing.
The spoiled boy-turned humble man
and the maid-turned CEO did find each other
and they married, but their marriage belly-flopped.
She married the idea of all the unfairness in this world in this world
under her thumb, over her lap.
He married the memory of someone caring
enough to correct his course. Wherever you go,
they are there, the luckless in love.
I can taste them on your tongue, answers to a question
I won't let myself ask. I kiss you harder as if to insist
that the boy didn't jump on the bed when the maid
told him not to, and I will never leave you, neither of us
will have a heart attack, ever, the sun resting
on our skin will never depart, leaving us cold in the dark,
and as for the black keys on the piano,
the minor notes, the weepy tones,
we'll pry them right off the keyboard.

MOONHANDLED

An 80-year-old woman enters Steak N'Shake,
orders black coffee, and beeps like Roadrunner
every time she needs a refill. The waitress sees
the surprise in my eyes, leans in, says, *Hon,*
she comes in here every full moon without fail.

The waitress's face is the wrinkled map
of one of those places everyone visits but no one
lives in. She makes me fall in love with her
loneliness, or maybe that's the moon. The
old woman beeps, bangs her empty cup

on the bar. I think I hear a coyote
among the wind-rattled trash cans.
The waitress and I agree that it's a lunatic world.
The day's headlines confirm it: *Thieves Lift*
Occupied Porta-potty! Hostage Fired for Missing Work!

She tells me about her son competing with
his college roommate over who could spit farthest
out their dorm window. The roommate thought
a running start would propel his spit a record distance,
but he tumbled out the window and landed before

the spit, which hit his face. *Full moon,* says
the waitress, *but he survived, and maybe it was*
the booze, not the moon, that made him do it. I tell her
about Li Po, who got drunk, tried to embrace
the moon's reflection in a lake, passed out,

and drowned. *Maybe the moon is really messing with us,*
I tell her. *Just in case,* I say, *let's take our biggest*
rockets and knock it down. She laughs.
I head for the lake, where I catch the moon
floating like a fat, pasty tourist

bobbing in an inner tube. I throw a rock at it
and yell "leave us alone!" But then a vision of
the world without the moon flashes, like
someone else's life, before my eyes, and it
looks something like *Invasion of the Body Snatchers*:

everyone the same, no one very interesting. Dear Lady,
those are my yellowed claws scratching your door,
that's my howl, my scritch, my panting in the night,
and this is my mange, my tangle of hair everywhere,
my belly itching for the ends of your nails.

WIVES OF THE POETS

Last week I told my class how Elinor Frost never forgave Robert
for little Elliot's death. She thought he didn't alert medics fast enough.
Maybe he took the road with too much traffic,
cracked a bearded, bespectacled young man,
or got lost in the beauty of the woods.
How can you joke about them losing a child?
accused a young woman with long earrings and boots,
and we launched into "Home Burial."

Flip a quarter and it's either an eagle flying
away as fast as it can or a dead president
trying to look dignified despite the worms
under his wig. This week I tell them
Wallace Stevens said *A poet looks at the world*
the way a man looks at a woman, but he
and his wife, Elsie, lived in separate sections of their house
and he never wrote her a love poem.
Thirteen ways of looking at a jackass,
murmurs the young woman, arms and brows crossed,
and the young man replies, *I'll bet he got tired of her*
getting on his case when he just wanted to unwind
with a little Guitar Hero, and I say, *We don't know*
much about his life, but…

It's fall semester, and as the trees bare themselves, the students
cover up and take back all the promises of spring
as the hot kisses they've planted on each other
ice over, and I know that next week when I tell them about
Williams Carlos Williams cheating on his wife, Flossie, these two
will say, *So much depends upon you flirting with my roommate,*
and *Not ideas about the cheapskate but the cheapskate himself.*

Today you broke the garage door and said I'm sorry.
You let the laundry pile up, and you're sorry.

Here I am airing our dirty laundry. I'm sorry,
you married a writer. All day I've planned my classes
and now I'm far away from you, lost in the woods of this poem,
which isn't great or maybe even good, and I'm sorry
that literary biographers and classrooms in the future
probably won't be discussing our marriage.
We're a sorry couple and no longer young,
but flip a coin a hundred times, and fifty times you'll forgive me,
and fifty times I'll tell you there's nothing to forgive.

PSALM ON A THEME BY DEAN YOUNG AND A SOMEWHAT SIMILAR THEME BY ALLEN GINSBERG

When I die, Lord, I want to come back
as a cloud an airplane passes through
just before the crash,
lit up by blazing sunset
and just freed of a heavy, cleansing rain—
a cloud gifted with speech
enough to say *Change your course, pilot.*
I want to change, cloudlike,
into the sort of person who finds a wallet
and an abandoned infant and knows which to keep,
which to return, and does it. Sometimes I lose myself
in a crowd. Sometimes I find myself
in a cloud. Sometimes I want to die, Lord,
from embarrassment. An expression
like *I'm falling apart* or *I love you to pieces,*
but if I do fall apart, Lord, I do
want you to love me to pieces.
It is written in a Dean Young poem,
The mind is a tiny island you've washed upon.
Is that true, Lord? About me, not you, I mean.
Dean Young the poet, not Dean Young the creator
of the comic strip, *Blondie,* I mean.
Allen Ginsberg wrote, *I'm sick of my own mind.*
Give me just a little piece of yours, Lord.
I'm going to give you a piece of my mind
is an expression, but I mean it literally.
I feel like a sandwich is an expression
meaning I crave bread and cheese
with ham/lettuce/mustard if you please,
but sometimes I do feel like Dagwood has
his eyes then his hands then his drooling mouth on me
and I feel like I know how Blondie must feel.
This makes me realize I don't want to die.

I've wandered forty years through the desert
of my mind, Lord. I want you to fill my mouth
with water and prayer and maybe a jagged little song.

SELF-PORTRAIT AS A CHILD'S STICK FIGURE DRAWING ON A REFRIGERATOR

"You are not what you think you are. You are something to be
imagined."—Clayton Eshleman

Often I'm a musical instrument
that's afraid of the sounds inside.
My days consist of arrayed efforts
not to hear or hum.
I'm like a baby who screams
at first seeing his arms swinging,
unaware those whips flung
straight at his head are attached to his body.
Why are you doing this to me?
a man asks his body as it fights sleep
and the crucial appendage droops after a woman
says *okay, why not*, after steak and lobster
and Sandra Bullock's latest formulaic schlock.
So spent, his body mocks him; he can't
fathom how he ever lifted the long-stemmed rose
he gave her, now drooping a little bit, too.
In my son's latest drawing labeled "Daddy,"
my hairs are stray spaghetti strands,
my head an oversized triangle crushing my stick-thin frame,
and a briefcase weighs down my three-fingered hand.
Often I feel sketchy like that, as if all the wrong colors
spill over my faint lines and anyone could cross me out
just like that. I haven't always felt like a stick figure.
I haven't always been an instrument
left forgotten in its case. I remember a time
in junior high when Doug Dickerson passed me
a pornographic flip book, the male stick figure's stick penis
getting bigger and bigger and the female stick figure's
stick legs getting farther and farther apart
until the stick figure bed broke and something hidden
deep inside me broke out, broke my body wide open,
a strange inchoate music that wanted to come out.

CONFESSIONS OF A FAILED BEATNIK

I'll admit that I shaved my scruff, patched my jeans
and then bought slacks, and what's more, a jacket, a tie,
and even shoes! matching, polished, and thus disguised,
I followed a trail of perfume that led, like a floral fluting
Pied Pieper, out of the Village, out of Manhattan even,
all the way to suburban Kentucky where I lost

myself, Man, where I forgot the words to every song
I'd ever sung to myself, let my dreams come unstitched,
Jack, quit drinking myself into nowhere Zen
stupors, and most afternoons, though not hungover,
I'm so headachy from meetings and emails
that I drive right past the brandy-colored light of

just-before sunset without pulling over to take it in,
then later rather than watching moonlight
illuminate the wind combing through unmown bluegrass,
I'm wiping kidpuke, there-there, I'm shining a flashlight
on the no-monsters under their bunk bed. I saw
the best minds of my generation toss aside their

necessary suffering, lose the art of losing, trade it all in
for golf clubs, I saw them trade the too-beautiful intensity
of feeling, feeling, feeling, for the calm comfort of
the girl-next-door's bare arms, and I'll admit I sold out, too,
and of late, no one has thought to compare me to a roman candle
exploding spider-like while everyone goes "awww!" No, far from it,

in fact, I mean dig this: one Fourth of July afternoon – not night –
I seared my foot on a sparkler, oh didn't I, the moral being:
don't wear sandals around any kind of lit fireworks, but
my kids were in an excited hurry so I did just that, and when
I showed them how to twirl the firey wire, a hot cherry landed
right underneath a strap and by the time I de-sandaled, my skin

was oozing fluids, but oh listen, Cats, my left hand didn't know
what my right hand was handing it when it offered a handshake
that turned out to be really a handcuff, yes I'll admit I put all
my pot pipes and tricyclics in a box, a mildewed cardboard box
I left in front of my mortgaged tract house with "Free" written
on the side in a pungent, licorice-smelling permanent ink smear,

and I'll be the first to admit that I'm not free, that I'll change
two diapers in the time it takes you to read this, that no
odor-proof pail will keep that stench from clinging
to my memory like tobacco to clothes at a dingy tavern,
Daddy-o, and I have to admit that I rarely visit dingy taverns
because my wife hates that smell and she makes me shower

afterwards, so standing here clean-shaven and cologned
and certifiably a carpooler and little-league coach, I hereby admit,
Angels, that I disgust myself, not like Robert Lowell as Peeping Tom
in "Skunk Hour" but more like a Benedict Arnold of Hiptown
turned double dealing traitor, citizen of Nowheresville. No need to point
fingers or a gun to my head, Doves, I'll freely admit that most full moons

I don't howl or chase cars, because I have to work the next morning,
and I'm not the kind of cat who wears women's underwear,
I've never leapt off a bridge, put my head in an oven,
attended a bullfight, shot my wife in the head while aiming
for an apple, carved my skin and called it research,
gone to prison (except to teach a poetry class), hitched cross

country, stepped in front of a car or tank or dune buggy,
or run for office just to write about it.
I don't even keep a bride on the side or any dark secrets
except those of my friends, most of whom are characters
in forgotten novels, and because this is a confessional poem
I'll admit that I'm pee-your-pants scared of my kids.

I mean like they pretend to be ghosts and I pretend to be scared,
right? But I really am scared, pretending not to be.
Scared they'll grow up to be like me in all the wrong ways.

Scared I'll run out of bread and they'll wear secondhand
sweaters, not bohemian chic tatters but real honest-to-Buddha
hand-to-mouth, sleeping-on-storm-grates poor. Scared they won't

grow up. Scared they'll grow up and I'll grow old, quick as
a car crash, and my poems will be totaled. Scared they'll turn
me into a piano, out of tune, dust on every key.

TURNING YOURSELF INTO THE WIND

I know you feel like no one
knows you. I understand
the long, disembodied slide
into the self-followed by the urge
to set off car alarms and toss
a garbage lid into the street.
The good news is you're coming together
like those leaves swirling in a column
and then forming a neat mound.
But you still feel invisible, don't you?
You're still the lone citizen
of your own ravenous body.
There you go, chasing after the parts of yourself
you've felt but never found. Bad news,
they've been watching you, the weathermen,
making their dire predictions. They're warning
your neighbors to hide in their basements
or lie flat in a ditch somewhere,
waiting it out while you rampage and rage.
Wouldn't it feel better to turn into music
or at least into words?

SCOTCH TAPE WORLD

Taping my thigh and calf together
at the knee, I contemplate taking
my children to Scotch Tape World,
where stars fall from the sky
like posters from my office door, where
the tires could fly off our car at
any moment. It's time they learn
that life is like that, that Disney lies
in the way of a true education. God
never lies, but He's still in trouble.
Why else would He have to clean
all the blackboards on which we
are unsolved math problems?
Our prayers go to Heaven, but first they go
through Scotch Tape World. Torn in transport,
they're pieced back together and presented
to God, who receives them as music
rather than as words. Holding your breath
waiting for people to be decent is one way
to go to God, who loves us just as He loves
the notes that David's harp wrote to Him.
Low clouds overhead seem to come
apart as if held together by cheap Scotch
tape. Such a pointless death, like the one
suffered by my first car, not to mention
Kenneth Patchen, who wrote "The animal
I wanted couldn't get into the world" and
other lines, penned, as Valery said, "by someone
other than the poet to someone other than
the reader." Our prayers might be missives
from someone other than us to someone
other than God. Behind my beard is a face
that's different from the one my wife married
years ago. Behind any given joke is the funk

that made us look for laughter. If you don't
know what I mean, you'll wake up one day
knowing. You'll look up and see sunlight hitting
a mountain so hard they both seem ready to shatter.

SLOW DANCE MUSIC

I can't explain the rain's attraction to my head,
though I'm touched by its desire to touch me.
I also can't explain unborn babies
sucking and blowing cigarettes bummed from

their young mothers, the absence of men from
the intricate inner worlds of their wives, or
the secret life of every dark street where
no one's wrist has the time. Help me

understand all the things that tumble from
the sky to the ground, from your eyes to
the corners of your mouth, from your mouth
to my ears, which are getting old, along with

the rest of me, for reasons no one has
adequately explained to me. Just when
I think I'm wearing a Tom Hunley mask
for a Halloween that never ends, I remember

that I know enough about how lost people can get,
how trapped in their own bodies and minds,
how much they resemble cattle strolling past
a huge hole in the fence, to know

I'll never understand this
music, which doesn't, after all, ask
for our understanding, only our bodies,
pressed together, swaying from side to side.

BIG NEWS
(After Tomaz Salamun)

Tom Hunley is one of the wild things
from *Where the Wild Things Are.*
Tom Hunley is the home run ball
people bite each other over in the cheap seats.
His favorite time of day is twilight, of course,
when everything is happening. Other people
and I, we pat him on the back when he walks by.
We buy him drinks. Why not? The world
is getting heavy with so many people
eating so many Big Macs, and sometimes
Tom Hunley acts like Atlas said
"Hold this" and then "Sucka!"

It used to be he could fly, they say,
but ex-girlfriends and other detractors
plucked his wings and showed them to him.
It used to be he could see, too, but
ex-girlfriends and other detractors plucked
his eyes, and for a second, he swears,
he could see himself perfectly.
This is all figurative, of course.
Tom Hunley taught that distinction
and so many others
to me and to so many others.

I've been following Tom Hunley on Twitter.
Today he's in Bowling Green, Kentucky.
Next week, maybe Fairmont, Minnesota,
City of Lakes. You can waterski there,
or snowmobile, and *don't forget your fishing pole!*
says Randy Quiring, Mayor. Next week
Tom Hunley and his sons plan to fly
a box kite in Fairmont, Minnesota,
and it will be big news there,
the wildest thing to hit Fairmont, Minnesota
since the grasshopper infestation of 1873.

MY WORST FEAR COMES TRUE

They change the English language, entirely,
while I sleep, announcing it bilingually
(Tom's English and New English)
on a social networking site
I don't know about. My job
as an English teacher is in peril.
If I say, *Do you have the time?* or
I'll have a double latte, please, the reply
might be *lightning hours* or *grey wind*.

I misread people's faces
because they've changed
body language, too.
Middle finger if you want the ketchup passed.
Pee dance upon greeting, instead of a handshake.

When I say *I love you*
to my beautiful wife
she calls the cops, because
those words no longer
mean what they used to mean.
A bilingual cop urges me to take
ESL and Body Language for Nobodies.
Instead of saying *I love the way your hair smells
and the sound of your breathing*, he instructs me
to say *avocado treefrog, honeyed sunlight*.
Instead of leaning in for a kiss, he says
I should use an old gang handshake, now used
by umpires to signal *safe at home*.

(from) Octopus (Logan House Press, 2008, winner of the Holland Prize)

THE DENTAL HYGIENIST

She said "open up,"
so I showed her my teeth,
a chipped-white fence
that keeps my tongue penned in.

She rinsed my mouth.
She suctioned my cheek.

She said "How do you like this town?"
so I said "Mmpllff,"
though I meant "More every day,"

and she said "Gorgeous weather!"
so I said "Mmpllff,"
though I meant "In my mouth?"

and she didn't say anything,
so I said "Mmpllff" and "Mmpllff"
though I'm not sure what I meant,
and she took me to mean
"Would you like to go out tonight?"
and "to an expensive restaurant?"

When I arrived with a bouquet of roses,
she stuffed them in my mouth.

She told me all about her feelings:
how she feels about fillings,
how she feels about failures.

She said "open up."
She said "It's like pulling teeth
trying to get men to talk about their feelings."

So I said " Mmpllff,"
though I meant "You smell prettier than the flowers in my mouth,"
and I said "Mmpllff,"
though I meant "I'm afraid of dying alone."

She said I was a good conversationalist
and showed me her perfect teeth.
I felt an ache in my jaw.
I felt drool crawling down my chin.

MUSIVES AND A QUIET CRUMP

Musive was a fine word, the name of a moth, gone extinct.
Crump: the sound of a heavy shell or bomb. *Hurkle*: a crouching,
cowering motion. *Erump*: to erupt, burst forth. Were these words
phased out, slow, or did they surface and then disappear
like whale backs? Maybe they entered and exited the language
in a rush, like *groovy*, *rad*, and *word up*, slang terms teens use,
then don't use, like a *rad hangout* turned into a *dork hub*
by the sudden arrival of parents. So many words,
but none for the smiles that flickered from Jane to me,

and back, when we'd reached a place in our life together
where we almost didn't need words. No word for
the strange joy I felt, cutting our firstborn son's umbilical cord
as he lay screaming on Jane's stomach. So many words,
but none tickled our infant son's throat. Jane
and I came to understand, this cry meant *I'm hungry*,
that one meant *burp me*, another meant *change me*.
Italians have seven words for "the," so why can't we
have words that distinguish a baby's different types of tears,

or a special word for the tears on Jane's face as she dug
her fingernails into her cheeks after he died in his crib?
Have you ever scratched someone, by accident,
as your arms grazed? I know the word for that. It's *scrazing*,
but I had no words to comfort Jane. *I'm sorry. It'll be okay.*
I knew these words didn't mean as much as I needed them to.
I had no words for the beasts eating my insides, musives
in a trunk full of clothes, no words for the hole I felt
and tried to fill with my writing, with my music,

with Camels and Jim Beam. And when Jane sought comfort
in another man's arms, when I found a red strand
of that man's hair on my pillow, on my bed,
when I was forced to imagine their wordless moans,
a quiet crump shocked my senses, left me hurkling, unable to erump.

The words *cuckold* and *how could you?* and *I'll kill him!*
weren't there for me. *Wife* and *son* had turned into archaisms.
I had nothing but my dictionary, which grunted, sighed, and shrugged,
a friend who had no words that could comfort me.

POEM

Outside
the window, Jane's
gone to war. An entire
world has been slammed shut, a coffin
lid, tight

(like my red-and-green Christmas tie, my Dali "Persistence of Memory"
tie, my literary tie with pictures of books on it, half-Windsor full-
Windsor I tug on it, let them drag me by it like a Dostoevskian beard,
yank it near off, and I know what Freud would say, prurient, perverted
Freud would ask and I would tell him, yes, my first time with Jane was
Jane's first time, bloody, tight)

as a
funeral drum,
tapping. Once I married
her. Here is our picture in the
paper

(the stained glass, the domed ceiling, her father walking her down
the aisle to Pachabel's Canon in D, the best man and groomsmen
all tuxedoed, a sworn secret society of vague evasions, neon haze of
Tequila, panties and pasties glowing green on stage, everything else
dark as the inside of a tomb, our son, too, a secret, hidden in Jane's
womb like an ounce of pot stowed in a glove compartment crossing the
border, our son, who already has crossed the border between this world
and the next, who haunts us now, chomps us with the ghost of his first
tooth, leaving marks only we can see, I wish I had a bullethole in my
belly, I could lift my tee shirt)

to prove
it. Now her legs
are as white as the dress
that she wore down the aisle that day,
because

(that morning she woke refreshed, grateful he finally slept through the
night, she absently unlatched the front of her nursing bra, yawned,
lifted him from his crib, tried to attach him to her, then seeing, fumbled
him back onto his little mattress, her first cigarette of the day, too,
falling, burning a hole in his blue blanket before I smashed the cherry-
end with my fist, and Jane finger-nailed her cheeks until blood streamed
out, and then for months, unable to enter his room, she begged me to
sell the house, to leave my job and this town, but I said I needed my
job, all the money I made)

she spent
the whole summer
immured in bed, grieving.
She's throwing rocks at the house. She's
leaving.

ELEGY FOR ROBERT CREELEY AND POPE JOHN PAUL II, DEAD THREE DAYS APART

Something dramatic is going to happen to me soon.
I feel myself and the whole world reset
to slow motion, and the hotel room I'm in
holds its breath. I see pigeons scatter
and clap their wings. I hear slow, operatic music,
and I feel scores of invisible fingers
fumbling at the threads that hold me together.

The black clouds outside are pregnant women
approaching labor, and as the sunspot
disappears from my carpet, I understand
that every godforsaken thing in this luminous world
will drift away, cloudlike;
as I slow-motion my way
to the window, the birds circle.

I see my hotel mirrored in the windows of another hotel,
and I see 10,000 people, vigilant outside my window.
They shout that I'm the next pope,
they toss up prayers and pigeons,
and a few detractors shout that I should jump.

The world speeds up again, like windswirling
leaves, and the crowd scatters in all directions
as if to say oh, you're a poet, not the pope, our mistake,
determined not to notice me, even while I open the window and
bellow:
my body is breaking down, too;
my spirit, too, will soon drift far, far off,
and all of you, too, you too.

Pope John Paul II, pray for us.
Robert Creeley too.

AT THE END OF A LONG AND VARIED CAREER

As a child, I rang doorbells and ran off,
leaving boxes full of electric rain clouds
and flaming bushes that recited verses.
When I grew up, I went into construction,
under-bid on a contract. Rebuild
the temple in three days?
I thought they'd crucify me then
and there, but I went bankrupt instead.
I took a teaching gig, had some luck
as a commercial fisherman. I lost
a bartending spot because I misunderstood
"Water down the wine." I became
a financial consultant, showed folks
how to stretch a little bread.
Resurrected! I am
in semi-retirement, unsure
what comes next. I've tried gardening before,
but I had a problem with snakes and weeds
that choked and poisoned my favorite flowers
and broke my heart. Now I'm taking up golf,
dimpling the world to my tee. "Fore!" I call,
but no one ducks and no one answers.
No one understands the word I'm saying,
just like they never understood the Word
that was, was with me, was me,
in the beginning. Let there be more
to eternity than morning-noon-night, repeat.
Than lather-rinse repeat. Than
wax-on, wax-off and still get beat up.
Let the sky fill with helium balloons,
brand new colors, and full-throated warblers,
brand new songs. So say I.

OCTOPUS

"I worked hard on that essay. Why did
    I get a 'C'?" the email read.
In reply, I described how hard I worked at tennis
    in my teens, Saturday nights spent
        sweating over my service motion. I could never place
        my shots as well as Andy Roddick, or hit at his pace.
Even if he were drunk, or had a broken leg, I couldn't test him.
            I asked this question:
    why couldn't they just give me
      a Wimbledon trophy
          for my hard work?
        I asked *Couldn't they grade on effort?*
But I deleted it, because this student wouldn't understand.
        Because I don't understand.
I never did make my mark as a tennis player,
    and, judging by my classrooms full of whining cheaters,
      I've failed just as spectacularly as a teacher.

This morning, between brewing and sipping my first cup of coffee,
    I changed my two-year-old's diaper, soothed him as he
        suffered the daily trauma of waking up
in a world that's way too big for both of us,
    prepped some rice cereal and a strawberry waffle
        for him and peeled a clementine and toasted a bagel
for my pregnant wife, who is on bed rest,
    wiped our son's mouth at her behest,
      loaded and unloaded the dishwasher,
    and took the garbage to the curb.

Tonight, as I sat, concentrating, in a stolen moment, on a blank page,
    I searched my brain for something to write about, a great
      epic subject to illuminate in a burst of song
      that would be so beautiful and true and strong
    that everyone would say "That Hunley has mastered this art;
            yes, he's really made his mark,"

85

but my son soon tricycled into my study, crawled
on my lap, spilled Gator Aid all
over my poem, and cried for my attention.
        I turned, defeated, and almost said to him:
        "You are part of the reason I can't find time to write.
        You are part of the reason I'm not living
        the kind of life that generates poetry.
        You are part of the reason I'm failing
        to make my mark."

But I didn't, because he wouldn't have understood.
    Or maybe because he would have understood.
        Then I remembered this scene from *The Octopus*, by
Frank Norris: an aspiring poet walks beside a train track, tries
    to think of a subject for his great epic of the American West.
        A flock of sheep charges through a broken fence,
    and the sheep don't stop to look both ways to avoid
the train. Amidst all that bleating and all that blood,
        the poet curses. His concentration has been
    shattered. He can't figure out how his poem will begin,
what it will be about, or how it will end.

ISM-ISM

You're not sure whether or not to divorce your spouse,
so you go for a walk to think-think-think, because
you're a thinker. A pair of bluebirds fly in unison, sing
in unison. They shoot straight up in unison and then,
as if in in a wordless, songless agreement to disagree, one
arcs sharp right, the other veers left at a mirror angle,
and because you're a Romanticist at heart, you decide
you have to break your marriage in half.
But you're part Postmodernist, too, so you think
maybe the birds are being ironic, and you think
staying and leaving are really just two ways
of doing the same thing. And since you're also
part Modernist, you pray, a throwback to your latent
Victorianism. You ask God what you should do, and
before He has a chance not to answer, you tell Him
you don't believe in him anymore, though at moments
like this, you wish to God you still did.

ECSTASY

At eighteen, when Frieda Lowe and I
split a heavy dose of impure X at a party,
Frieda lifted her knees to her chest
and wrapped them in her arms, as if
her ribs needed a second cage to keep
her heart from flying away.

    Love, I think I'm hallucinating
    when I watch our firstborn belly-surf
    on a rainbow-shaped pillow
    as I rock his baby brother to sleep.

Leaving the party, Frieda and I parted for
good. She tripped down a cliff.
Hospital. Stomach pump. I
broke down and directed traffic, after a
lady cop, at the end of her shift, handed me
some flares, and said *good luck*.

    I'm flashing back to a night when
    raindrops crashed on the roof of this
    home we part own, part owe on. A sliver
    of moonlight through the curtain
    showed me your naked body.

The flares streaked across the sky like bolt lightning.
I waved them in all directions and believed in God
racing through my bloodstream. I kept
believing until I fell down hard, got caught.
Psych ward. County detox. Rehab. Jail.
Forty days and nights inside the flood.

    When lightning bit the sky that night,
    rain stopped falling all at once,
    replaced by the moans of crickets.
    Our bodies coming together were
    a song of hope the moonlight sang to the darkness.

OUT OF BODY EXPERIENCES

I wanted out of my body, so I flew
into the body of a bird, a canary,
but then my canary heart beat
1,000 times per minute. It felt
like fifty Red Bulls all at once.
My heart wasn't used to so much
fluttering, so much frantic singing.
I wanted out, so I dive-bombed into
Giovanni Verrazano, who discovered
the Hudson River before Henry Hudson,
who got all the credit. In this new body,
I was glad to be a man again, proud of
my discovery but envious of Henry Hudson,
whose name would be immortalized by a
historical error, the way the French Horn
was actually invented in Germany.
I wished I could be the embodiment
of such mistaken immortality.
I wished to be Henry Hudson.
I wanted the credit, not the accomplishment,
so I flew into Henry Hudson's body
and felt satisfied for a moment,
but there was a crew uprising and I was left
in a rowboat, to die in the very river
that would take my name. In that moment,
I wished I had a carrier pigeon, so I could send
my apologies to my noble rival, Giovanni Verrazano.
I wanted to tell him I knew I was the true also-ran,
like Samuel Langley, second to fly, after the Wright brothers,
or Elisha Grey, who tried to patent the telephone
on 2/14/1876, hours after Alexander Graham Bell
left the patent office, whistling like a bird, like a ringing phone.
Wishing I could leave my body without dying first,
I swam into the body of a female blue whale.
My heart weighed fifteen hundred pounds.

My heavy heart was an anchor capable of plunging me
into fathomless depths and I had a sudden urge
to nestle up against a bull whale and open myself
to his massive phallus, which isn't much odder
than Rene Descartes' fetish for cross-eyed girls
or Charles Baudelaire's love for Squint-eyed Sarah,
the prostitute who gave him syphilis. I wished
to be a man again, a smart and accomplished man,
but not Descartes or Baudelaire. I wished I could be
William Shakespeare, and hallelujah! I flew
into William Shakespeare. William Shakespeare
of the Kalamazoo Shakespeares, who invented
a revolutionary new fishing reel. An accomplished man
whose name would never be forgotten, I knew
I could die satisfied, and I wished my heart
would become a bird and fly, singing, out of my mouth.

IN PRAISE OF PUDDLES

Legless, unarmed, without
muscular bodies or the power
of the exclamation "Oh Lord,
how thy wisdom hast formed us all!"
they work, they fill up.

They reflect the most fragile branches,
mirror the wispiest clouds.

Ugly kid sisters and understudies
to the mighty rivers great poets praise,
they attract our unready shoes or

our jeans and sweaters as we tumble,
too keen on embracing the moment
to notice the little worlds we've entered.

INTERDISCIPLINARY STUDIES

A poet's words could be pulled apart
and the letters reassembled
into copy for a beer commercial,
and this is called literary criticism.

A nation could be taken apart
like an engine and rebuilt
using imported parts,
and that is called political science.

My house could be broken apart
and burned to warm the homeless —
which would then include me —
and that is called economics.

Your emotions could be torn apart,
and a shrink could make you paint
your severed ear the deepest blue ever seen,
and that is called oceanography, or psychology, or art history.

Then you could ask me
"What is the meaning of all this?"
and that's philosophy,

and I would reply
"God, I don't know,"
which, some days, is all the theology I can muster.

(from) The Tongue (Wind Publications, 2004)

GUNMAN IN CONTEXT

A gunman entered the Ditto, a bar filled with typewriters.
He robbed the register. I typed "ohmanagunohgodagunman"
and I liked the feel of it on my fingers,
the sense of power, like pulling a trigger.

If I saw him, say, on a city bus, sans gun,
he'd have seemed like just another man,
and we'd have talked loaded decks, loaded questions,
all the loads he carries alone. We'd have talked
broken promises and glasses, all the brokenness
that provides ammunition for his anger.

The gun in his hand made him a gunman.
Then again, he could have held it anywhere.
Gun in his teeth? Gunman.
Gun concealed like a wallet in his pants? Gunman.
Sitting in church, praying, gun immured in the sanctum
of his boots, he would have been a gunman,
and this is the part we fail to understand.

We understand a gunman at a bank or at 7-11,
but what about a lone gunman, pursuing
a gunwoman through the personals?
And maybe this is the problem: we don't think
of the gunman until he has the gun in his hand.

Imagine a gunman in the second person: "you are a gunman,"
or in the subjunctive: "if he were a gunman,"
or in the imperative: "put down your gun, man."
The gunman at the Ditto got shot,
a dead man landing, unhanding his gun.

JUBILATE LEO
After Christopher Smart

I will consider the MGM lion.
For I am allergic to the dander of house cats,
but I love the movies.
For he eats box office receipts and for two hours at a time
he tears at the flesh of our boredom and pain.
For the first time I saw him I spilled the popcorn of my worries
all over the rolling reel of my darkness.
For he has seen God, once in color and once in black and white.
For he is of the line of the lions who spared Daniel in the den.
For millions of teenage girls think Leonardo DiCaprio
is King of the Jungle but I say
he's just the clown with his head in the tolerant lion's mouth.
For his fur is yellow but even the baddest Bart of all blackhatted cinema outlaws
won't call <u>him</u> yellow.
For at the end of the yellow brick road he regained his courage.
For his motto "Ars Gratia Artis" was shared by Oscar Wilde, Dostoevsky, Jane
Austen, Marilyn Monroe, Cary Grant, Buster Keaton,
and all of the truly faithful.
For he always lands on all fours.
For he makes us believe that we can knock down or open any door.
For in our seats we only whisper, and leave it to him to roar.

MORSELS, REMORSE, MORTE

It's Easter Sunday and we're watching *Jesus Christ Superstar*,
and there's a woman on my couch; she's 29 and beautiful,
but nostalgic about being 19 and irresistible. She's eating
cheesecake and her face is beatific like the face
of the resurrected Jesus when he appears to Mary Magdelene,
who, in the movie, is both beautiful and irresistible,
with a sonorous voice that could make statues of angels

weep blood, and the woman on my couch says
"I wish I could stay eternally in the state
of eating this cheesecake," while Mary Magdelene sings
"Everything's all right, yes, everything's fine," but then
the woman on my couch calculates the damage: 550 calories
and 32 grams of fat = 300 stomach crunches
and an hour on the treadmill, and her cheesecake-induced

ecstatic glow turns at once to the look Judas gets
later in the evening, right before he tosses away
his ill-gotten silver, sings, and hangs himself,
though the rope fits loosely, and if I didn't know
how the story ends, I'd wonder whether he'd be able
to pull it off. That selfsame look betrays me

every time I try to fall out of love, which is like
trying to fall headfirst out of a deep hole or
like that woman trying to return to a time when her
presence on the beach made men forget the waves
and their wives or like Judas looking for a way
to spend the thirty pieces of silver he got
in exchange for the fractured remains of his soul.

BIOLOGY

means "study of life,"
if you look at its roots,
but Ron Rice, my lab partner in tenth grade,
just wanted to look at
his pot stash under the microscope.

He swore he could see
the THC, but all I saw
were red strands roping
around hard green buds,
and crystals shining like dimes
on a sunlit tennis court.

People liked to call Ron "Rat."
He had a rat-tail in his hair
like the guys in Duran Duran.
He had a turned-up nose that twitched
whenever he had an itch, and if
you put him under a microscope,

you'd have seen that
he would steal your jacket,
pawn it to buy coke,
and then help you look for it.
Our senior year, Ron OD'd and died
— suicide —

and everyone forgot
that they'd ever called him "Rat."
They eulogized him and cried.
Man, if you were to look
at one of those tears
under a microscope,

you'd see something human
dog-paddling and gasping its last,
and you'd see something inhuman
holding it down, drowning it.

MORNING SONG

I awoke from a dream
in which I was Gilligan
and you were both Ginger
and Mary Ann, but rather
than Gilligan, I was the professor,
and rather than Ginger
and Mary Ann, you were a band
of natives, brandishing spears,
and I saw the raft that I designed
shrinking under the sun.

I awoke in your arms,
but rather than your arms,
I was in a cathedral,
and rather than a pew,
I sat in a Jeep Cherokee.
You and I were at the drive-inn,
making out on the bench seat,
while the minister droned
from the silver screen.

I awoke and saw myself
in your eyes, but far
from being in your eyes,
I was in a maple tree,
in a cemetery,
in 1929.
I was birdsong,
you were echo,
and the tombstones
rattled with longing.

I awoke beside you,
but rather than being beside you,
I was beside myself,

in Noah's Ark, the rest
of creation waking, two-by-two,
and I swore I'd trade
the male of each species
for one of your kisses.
You became a dove,
I, an olive branch in your beak,

and we awoke
at a dance hall in Heaven,
where God sneaked
nectar into the punch,
and kept trying
to cut in on me.

MY FIRST CAR

My first car could go from zero to sixty in five seconds flat.

It had no get-up-and-go but I used to cruise the streets in it all night long.

There was a teen curfew in my town and I was sixteen, so I never dared drive after eight.

I had just turned eighteen and I loved pulling into convenience stores,
         ecstatic about buying cigarettes legally;
               I would smoke and speed and flick ashes out the window
                  and kiss my girlfriend while driving through tunnels;

My girlfriend never kissed me because cigarettes made my breath stink –
      "like sucking an exhaust pipe," she said.

She wasn't really my girlfriend. She was just using me
      for rides in my convertible speedster.

My car was a VW Beetle. It could barely do fifty, plus it was starting to stink,
      like my breath from the constant smoking.

I never took up smoking because my parents are always telling me
      about my granddad's death from lung cancer when I was four.

I don't know what my parents are talking about.
      I have dinner with my granddad every Sunday.

I never knew my parents. They died when I was eight, but they left me
      a trust fund that paid for my first car.

I tell you truly I never had a car at all.

I'm a big liar cruising past you
      with a banner on the door that says "Vote for Hunley!"

You can trust me.

FAMOUS POET

I've been dead for fifteen   years
from now I'll finally have the recognition I deserve
to have articles written about   my oeuvre
has inspired   more than one younger poet
has become a yale younger poet by penning elegies
          and half truths
mark the three new biographies   people wrote about me
and got the facts   wrong
or right my poems were not about   my life
went by too quickly and too slowly at the same   time
is a strange chain I'm glad to have broken   it
turns out they're finally giving me   a Pulitzer
can set a poet up for life   and death
is a cushy residency   a distinguished chair
in the back of the room   is the only one   empty
words boom from the microphone at the tribute   reading
from my poems my friends really show   my critics
say my death was a brilliant career   move
it's hard to see the podium from here

THE MAN WHO WAS SMARTER THAN HIMSELF

There was a man who was smarter than himself
by a full twenty IQ points, who kept swindling himself
in high stakes solitaire games, baffling himself

with his logic, and letting himself copy
his college homework. One day, having lunch by himself,
he looked up from his Baudrillard and muttered to himself

about the pretensions of others, but he caught himself
not paying attention. He caught himself
staring, through the corner of a strained eye,

at a woman who was eating by herself.
She was more beautiful than herself
as she cringed into a mirror and called herself a Pimply Patty.

"Are you listening to me?" the man asked himself,
but he heard himself say "You're not so smart,"
and he watched himself straighten his tie,

clear his throat, and approach the woman,
and he debated with himself
over the right words to say.

HOW TO MAKE ORANGE JUICE

First you have to make the oranges.
To do that you must become
an orange tree, which means moving
to Florida or Southern California.
If you go to San Diego, the beach
will beckon you, with its bikinis
and its waves, and you will feel the temptation

to take up surfing, which would get in the way
of becoming an orange tree. Stay focused
on your goals. Visualize all things orange:
carrots bursting from the ground,
a field of poppies blossoming all
at once, like some unplanned party,
a haunted house peopled by jack-o-lanterns.
Eat only the orange M&M's
in each packet. Make friends only

with redheads. Concentrate entirely
on orange juice, which is not the same
as buying orange juice made from concentrate.
Stop looking for the easy way.

GOD IN THE CHEESE

Three Trappist monks from Gethsemane, Kentucky
    are being interviewed on Channel 6 news.
The monks make their living by making cheese,
    and their cheese is making them famous.
"How do you manage to make such wonderful cheese?" mumbles
    the newsman, his cheese-packed mouth grinning beatifically.
"We really put our souls into the process," says one.
    "Making cheese is a form of prayer for us," says the next.
"We find God in the cheese," says the third.

Right off I think of Hindus, who find not God but gods,
    and see the sacred not in processed cheese
but in the grazing cow itself. Hindu fakirs have stared
    at the sun and gone blind, and they've held their arms
above their heads until the arms withered, going to extremes
    because of their extreme hunger for enlightenment.
The news also makes me think of Richard of Chichester,
    disciplined medieval scholar, who shared a robe with two hovel-mates.
One would wear the robe and attend a lecture, while the others
    would stay in the hovel, freezing, strapped for cash,
starving students in the school of hunger, hankering for hunks of cheese.

All of this fills me with shame, because I'm watching the news
    on Channel 6 when I'm supposed to be studying with monkish rigor.
I do take consolation, though, in remembering Louis Pasteur,
    who taught us how to pasteurize cheeses and other perishable foods
because Napoleon III asked him to investigate diseases that were killing
    the Paris wine industry. See, before he invented pasteurization,
not to mention the anthrax and rabies vaccines, Louis Pasteur preferred
    the indolent occupations of fishing and painting to boning up
for his chemistry exams. Becoming more focused, he said,
    "In the fields of observation, chance favors only the prepared mind"
which is another way of saying "We find God in the cheese."

Thinking so much about cheese awakes a hunger in me.
As I head towards my refrigerator, I think of the Salvation Army,
how the unshaven and unshowered, desperate for a meal, must sit through sermons
    before they may eat. After two hours on those hard pews, surely
    they find God in the cheese. I open my refrigerator and find
    a forgotten block of pepperjack cheese. I turn it around,
looking for God in the cheese, and I realize there's a big difference
    between finding God in the cheese when you're making the cheese
and finding God in the cheese when you're eating the cheese,
    so I say a little prayer, "God, get out of there!"
as I camel my back and begin nosing and eyeballing the cheese.
    I really believe that He's there, but all I find is a coat of green and white mold.
As I throw the cheese in the garbage, I feel my chest swell up with sighs,
    and I watch the whole kitchen fill with the glow of my hunger.

(from) Still, There's a Glimmer (Wordtech Editions, 2004)

STILL, THERE'S A GLIMMER,

a strand of sunlight
striking the torn
pages of us, glitter
on the thawing
lake of us, and yeah

the newspapers will keep saying
what they've been saying,
and we don't deny
the thick darkness of us
where the smarter part of us
tries to hide,

and we don't pretend
that on a summer day,
a whisk of perfume
can't thrust us into
an inconsolable grief,
until part of us floats away
never to return,

while another part,
pitched headlong
into the gummiest of circumstances,
seeks asylum,
and we don't try to tune out
the thrum of the chafing
orchestra of us,

but oh there are new wonders
smeared on every sidestreet,
dollar bills to find,
outbreaks of pine cones,
birthmarks on the cheeks
of pretty faces, and the sound

of babies kicking reminds us
that for each one of us
breathing dreamers,
there are billions of cells
that never got the chance
to be even a little immortal.

THE FIRE REMEMBERS JOAN OF ARC

I wanted to touch her gently,
and then to enter her—a lover,
I, and all those shepherd boys of Domremy,
I, and all those soldiers fighting for her flag.
"Forgive me, Maid of Orleans,"
I roared before I licked her ankles. "It's
my nature to destroy the ones
who come too close to me."

She said "Your flames won't singe my cross" and held
two twigs against her breast. She said
"a cloud of angels told me so."
I laughed, a sad, involuntary crackle,
and suddenly she wore the face
of a naive teenage seamstress, not
the mighty visage of the general
who led the charge against the English Lion.

I wrapped around the makeshift cross,
but Saint Joan's angels told the truth:
her cross stood strong. Joan began to burn,
and she prayed for Bishop Cauchon,
the hypocrite who tried her as a witch.
She prayed for her Dauphin, the spineless man
she crowned. She prayed for England, her enemy
who demanded ransom, for her beloved France
who wouldn't pay, and for every back-scratching,
courtroom-entrapping, money-grubber in the crowd.

Enraged, I wanted to run through the street, raze
their church, their homes, the entire city of Rouen.
I stayed to touch her gently
and shield her from the crowd.
She shrieked "Don't think I blame you, Fire.
You can't help it that you're so hot,"
and she was right. I couldn't help myself.
Becoming large, I entered her, ravaged her, loved her.

SORRY TO SAY "NO THANK YOU"

Dear Madam or Sir:
Dear Poet:
Dear Submitter:

We hate form rejection slips, too.

Thanks for letting us see your work.
Thanks for your interest.
Thanks for the submission.
Thanks for the interesting submission.

Not this time. I'm sorry,
but we're stocked for at least
the next two years, or more.
None of these fit with our current issue.

We were so impressed with the high quality of the manuscripts we received,
we're convinced that many of them are sure to find publishers in the near future.
We salute you for continuing to write in a world that provides so many
almost convincing reasons not to.
Unfortunately, we are returning your submission unread. Our next two issues
are editorially complete.

I liked the Buk poem, though — it was a close call.
In our estimation, your style is appropriate for publication. Please do submit again
Our present theme is "Family: Tradition & Responsibility."
You have a knack for "following through" by staying with the unfurling stages
of transformation; very gritty, very nice.
Your work is honest. Please send us more later.

They don't quite fit in but they do
have a nice humorous quality.
Your poems seem to be a little self-consciously poetic.

Would you be interested in a subscription swap
for the magazine you edit?
We urge you to buy and read at least one issue.
Your piece was really interesting but we're not accepting anything
but subscriptions.

Very nice. Sorry, but we no longer publish.
We are on the fritz. Not dead, just on hiatus.
We're not doing another issue. I bought a bike instead!

I'm glad you're "out there."
It was good to hear from you. These aren't right for us.
Good luck in finding homes for your poems.

MINIMALIST LOVE STORY

Me, hugging the wall like ivy.   Her, decked out in a yellow mini-skirt, dancing. Me, practicing my line like a bit part actor.   Her, resting her tiny feet. Me, swigging on my Yukon Jack, spraying Binaca into my mouth, sauntering up to her. Me and her dancing? Me and her dancing! ... Me and her at her door. Me and her in her room? Her in her room. Me on the porch. Me and her phone number on her porch. Me and her phone number and a jack-o-lantern grin...Me and a rose. Me blushing and the rose blushing. Her blushing. Me and her and the rose, all blushing. The rose and water. Meandher! Herandme! The rose and water. Her and me. Me and her. Her and a day job. The rose wilting. Me.   Her.

Me and someone else. Meandsomeoneelse. Her? Her!
Me   Someone else. Meandherandsomeoneelse? ... Her and someone else, dancing. Me, glued to the wall like a poster. Me and my Yukon Jack. Me and the florist and a dozen roses. Her and a dozen roses. Me and her porch. The flung roses and a slamming door.

Herandsomeone else.   Me and the personal ads.

THE FIRST TIME WE KISSED

The last time I sighed I
expelled a large family
of Lilliputian migrant workers
from my mouth. One of them explained
that the clouds foretold a great tornado
accompanied by thunder and lightning.
"Until she blows over, you're our shelter,"
he said, as they climbed
back into my mouth.

The last time you laughed
a v-shaped choir of Canadian geese
sprang like a song from your lips.
You asked how they got there,
but they spoke no English. They just
honked a hymn at the heavens,
and with their wings they made a wind
like breath, and as you inhaled again
they flew back into your mouth.

The first time we kissed
our hearts
thundered.
I saw lightning
in your eyes,
I heard Canadian geese
fluttering their wings,
I heard a migrant
worker say:
"This isn't so bad.
This isn't so bad
after all."

INTERCOURSE

As we made love, our scars met,
grazing long enough for mine to say
"He tries to hide me,"
and for yours to reply
"I know I embarrass her."

"He never learned how to swim," whispered my scar.
"She got picked last in gym class,
then cried in the locker room," replied yours.

Just then, a huge wound opened in me.
You touched it. It closed.
I was filled, fully healed, and I knew
I would never be able not to love you.

ACKNOWLEDGMENTS

The following poems appeared in *Adjusting to the Lights*, winner of the 2020 Rattle Chapbook Prize: "Dear God, Show Me How To Walk In Wonder"; "A World Inside This World"; "The Last Time I Took My Son To The Movies"; "What She Said"; "Remember Those Girls, Lord"; "What Feels Like Love"; and "Pounds".

These poems were previously published in literary journals. Thanks to the editors.

5 AM: "Morsels, Remorse, Morte"

A Narrow Fellow: "Surrounded By Aliens"

The American Journal of Poetry: "Will Be Done"

American Poetry Journal: "At the End of a Long and Varied Career"

Anti-: "Um"

Anti-Heroin Chic: "Pounds"

Apalachee Review: "Gunman in Context" and "How to Make Orange Juice"

Atlanta Review: "Turning Yourself Into the Wind"

Atticus Review: "Goodnight Milhouse"

Chiron Review: "Morning Song" and "What Feels Like Love"

Cimarron Review: "The Man who was Smarter than Himself"

Crab Creek Review: "Otto Mann, Intrepid Bus Driver" and "Biology"

Crab Orchard Review: "Officer Down (Chief Clancy Wiggum)"

Crazyhorse: "The Last Time I Took My Son To The Movies"

decomP magazinE: "Watch Tom Freeze To Death"

Diode Poetry Journal: "Edna Krabappel"; "Lisa Simpson—'Jihadist Homer'"; and "Wives of the Poets"

Exquisite Corpse: "Minimalist Love Story"

Green Hills Literary Lantern: "The Dental Hygienist"

Gumball Poetry: "How to Make Orange Juice"

Hampden-Sydney Poetry Review: "God in the Cheese"

Hawai'i Review: "Sorry to Say 'No Thank You'"

Heliotrope: "My First Car"

Jeopardy: "The First Time We Kissed"

Los Angeles Review: "Out of Body Experiences"

MARGIE: "Big News"

Michigan Quarterly Review: "Dear God, Show Me How To Walk In Wonder"

National Poetry Review: "Self-Portrait as a Child's Stick Figure Drawing on a Refrigerator"

New Orleans Review: "Slow Dance Music"

New South: "Troy McClure"

New York Quarterly: "Ism-Ism"

North American Review: "Moonhandled"

North Dakota Quarterly: " World Inside This World"

Paddlefish: "Confessions of a Failed Beatnik"

Perspectives (A Journal of Reformed Thought): "Psalm on a Theme by Dean Young and a Somewhat Similar Theme by Allen Ginsberg"

Poems & Plays: "My Worst Fear Comes True"

Poetry East: "Elegy for Robert Creeley and Pope John Paul II, Dead Three Days Apart"; "How to Make Orange Juice"; "Intercourse"; and "Morning Song"

Rattle: "Moe Szyslak" and "Here Lies Tom C. Hunley, On His Hammock"

Red Earth Review: "Here Lies Tom C. Hunley, who, according to the coroner"

Reunion (The Dallas Review): "Tom Ignored The Warning Labels"

River Styx: "Poem"

The Scream: "Scotch Tape World"

Shift: A Journal of Literary Oddities: "Watch Tom Hunley Freeze To Death"

Slippery Elm: "Here Lies Tom C. Hunley, killed in a car wreck" and "Tom's Death With A David Bowie Soundtrack"

Smartish Pace: "Herman Hermann, Owner of Herman's Military Antiques"

Southern Indiana Review: "Interdisciplinary Studies"

Southern Poetry Review: "Jubilate Leo (Rejoice in the Lion)"

Story South: "Elegy for Robert Creeley and Pope John Paul II, Dead Three Days Apart" and "The Fire Remembers Joan of Arc"

Texas Review: "Ecstasy"

TriQuarterly: "Musives and a Quiet Crump"

Valparaiso Poetry Review: "Um"

Verse Daily: "At the End of a Long and Varied Career"; "Slow Dance Music"; "Self-Portrait as a Child's Stick Figure Drawing on a Refrigerator"; and "Surrounded By Aliens"

Verse Wisconsin: "Psalm on a Theme by Dean Young and a Somewhat Similar Theme by Allen Ginsberg"

Virginia Quarterly Review: "In Praise of Puddles"

The Volta: "Big News"

Waxwing: "Prayer Asking For Patience And Compassion"

Windhover (A Journal of Christian Literature): "Here Lies Tom C. Hunley, On His Hammock"

Wordgathering (A Journal of Disability Poetry and Literature): "What She Said"

The Writer's Almanac with Garrison Keillor: "The Dental Hygienist"

Xavier Review: "Famous Poet"

Zone 3: "What Can Be Said about the Beautiful-from-a-Distance Elegant Etcetera in the Broken Syllables of Our Imperfect Tongues?"

C&R PRESS TITLES

NONFICTION
Women in the Literary Landscape by Doris Weatherford, et al
Credo: An Anthology of Manifestos & Sourcebook for Creative
Writing by Rita Banerjee and Diana Norma Szokolyai

FICTION
Last Tower to Heaven by Jacob Paul
History of the Cat in Nine Chapters or Less by Anis Shivani
No Good, Very Bad Asian by Lelund Cheuk
Surrendering Appomattox by Jacob M. Appel
Made by Mary by Laura Catherine Brown
Ivy vs. Dogg by Brian Leung
While You Were Gone by Sybil Baker
Cloud Diary by Steve Mitchell
Spectrum by Martin Ott
That Man in Our Lives by Xu Xi

SHORT FICTION
Fathers of Cambodian Time-Travel Science by Bradley Bazzle
Two Californias by Robert Glick
Notes From the Mother Tongue by An Tran
The Protester Has Been Released by Janet Sarbanes

ESSAY AND CREATIVE NONFICTION
Selling the Farm by Debra Di Blasi
the internet is for real by Chris Campanioni
Immigration Essays by Sybil Baker
Death of Art by Chris Campanioni

POETRY

What Feels Like Love by Tom C. Hunley

The Rented Altar by Lauren Berry

Between the Earth and Sky by Eleanor Kedney

What Need Have We for Such as We by Amanda Auerbach

A Family Is a House by Dustin Pearson

The Miracles by Amy Lemmon

Banjo's Inside Coyote by Kelli Allen

Objects in Motion by Jonathan Katz

My Stunt Double by Travis Denton

Lessons in Camoflauge by Martin Ott

Millennial Roost by Dustin Pearson

All My Heroes are Broke by Ariel Francisco

Holdfast by Christian Anton Gerard

Ex Domestica by E.G. Cunningham

Like Lesser Gods by Bruce McEver

Notes from the Negro Side of the Moon by Earl Braggs

Imagine Not Drowning by Kelli Allen

Notes to the Beloved by Michelle Bitting

Free Boat: Collected Lies and Love Poems by John Reed

Les Fauves by Barbara Crooker

Tall as You are Tall Between Them by Annie Christain

The Couple Who Fell to Earth by Michelle Bitting

Notes to the Beloved by Michelle Bitting